MORE FREAKY SCIENCE DISCOVERIES

BY SARAH MACHAJEWSKI

Gareth Stevens
PUBLISHING

Please visit our website, www.garethstevens.com. For a free color catalog of all our high-quality books, call toll free 1-800-542-2595 or fax 1-877-542-2596.

Library of Congress Cataloging-in-Publication Data

Names: Machajewski, Sarah, author.
Title: More freaky science discoveries / Sarah Machajewski.
Description: New York : Gareth Stevens Publishing, [2020] | Series: Freaky true science | Includes index.
Identifiers: LCCN 2018060869| ISBN 9781538240588 (paperback) | ISBN 9781538240601 (library bound) | ISBN 9781538240595 (6 pack)
Subjects: LCSH: Discoveries in science–Juvenile literature.
Classification: LCC Q180.55.D57 M325 2020 | DDC 500–dc23
LC record available at https://lccn.loc.gov/2018060869

First Edition

Published in 2020 by
Gareth Stevens Publishing
111 East 14th Street, Suite 349
New York, NY 10003

Designer: Sarah Liddell
Editor: Therese Shea

Photo credits: Cover, pp. 1 (tardigrade), 7 3Dstock/Shutterstock.com; cover, p. 1 (microscope and cylinder used throughout book) Morphart Creation/Shutterstock.com; background used throughout andrey_l/Shutterstock.com; hand used throughout Helena Ohman/Shutterstock.com; paper texture used throughout Alex Gontar/Shutterstock.com; p. 5 Kristina Yu/Shutterstock.com; p. 9 Emil Von Maltitz/Oxford Scientific/Getty Images; p. 11 Scharfsinn/Shutterstock.com; p. 13 jeafish Ping/Shutterstock.com; p. 15 VCG/Contributor/Visual China Group/Getty Images; p. 17 photo courtesy of NASA; p. 19 ADRIAN DENNIS/Staff/AFP/Getty Images; p. 21 GliderMaven/Wikimedia Commons; p. 23 (diagram) VectorMine/Shutterstock.com; p. 23 (northern lights) Jamen Percy/Shutterstock.com; p. 25 (jellyfish) Ssblakely~commonswiki/Wikimedia Commons; p. 25 (GFP) Nine Yossakorn/Shutterstock.com; p. 27 Jeffrey Coolidge/The Image Bank/Getty Images; p. 29 (ISS) Vadim Sadovski/Shutterstock.com; p. 29 (flatworm) Esv/Wikimedia Commons.

Printed in the United States of America

CPSIA compliance information: Batch #CS19GS: For further information contact Gareth Stevens, New York, New York at 1-800-542-2595.

CONTENTS

Words in the glossary appear in **bold** type
the first time they are used in the text.

NOT SCIENCE FICTION

What secrets lie in the far reaches of a science lab? Look in one tank and you'll find a two-headed worm. Across the room, a potato is powering a light bulb. And that's to say nothing of the glowing cells growing in dishes around the corner. These freaky findings sound like scenes from a science fiction novel, but there's nothing fictional about them. These are real science discoveries—of the freakiest kind.

Science discoveries happen all the time, and often by accident. Scientists set out to investigate one thing and end up stumbling upon something strange and sometimes useful—like X-rays and the microwave oven. One thing is certain: when it comes to science, things can get pretty weird!

FREAKY FACTS!

Science is important to all kinds of industries, including medicine, farming, and music. You can't escape science!

THE SCIENTIFIC METHOD

Science is all about finding out answers to questions big and small. Why does the weather change? How can one car travel faster than another? No matter what you're asking, the scientific method is a tool you can use to get the answer. It's a series of steps that help you focus on a question, develop a **hypothesis**, conduct an experiment to test it, **analyze** your findings, and come to a conclusion. Test again to make sure you're right!

WEIRD THINGS GO DOWN IN SCIENCE LABS ALL OVER THE WORLD. IT'S WHERE SCIENCE COMES TO LIFE!

THE ANIMAL THAT WILL OUTLIVE HUMANS

Tardigrades are tiny, scrunched-up animals with eight legs. They may be very small and very weird looking, but they're fierce. They can survive the harshest conditions, even in outer space! In fact, it's likely they'll outlive humans.

Research shows that tardigrades can survive temperatures as cold as –328°F (–200°C) and as hot as 300°F (149°C). They can survive exposure to toxic materials, boiling liquids, and high levels of pressure. They can even live in space without a spacesuit. You can't say the same for humans!

Scientists recently discovered that these tiny tanks would survive an asteroid hitting Earth and other events that could bring about the end of the human race. Thanks to tardigrades, life would go on.

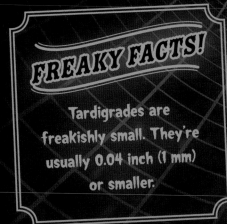

FREAKY FACTS!

Tardigrades are freakishly small. They're usually 0.04 inch (1 mm) or smaller.

TARDIGRADES, ALSO CALLED WATER BEARS AND MOSS PIGLETS, HAVE SHORT, STUMPY LEGS. THEY USE THEIR HIND LEGS, WHICH ARE BACKWARD, TO GRASP THINGS.

THE TRUTH ABOUT TARDIGRADES

Discovered in 1773, there are more than 1,000 species of tardigrades. Tardigrades endure extreme conditions because their bodies go into a special survival state. When exposed to a threat, a tardigrade curls into a dried-out ball, called a tun, and its body's activity levels drop. The tun protects the tardigrade from ice, low oxygen levels, and the freezing cold. Experiments have brought tardigrades back to life after years as a tun!

ZOMBIE CATERPILLARS

Some caterpillars face an enemy worse than death. It's a virus that invades them, controls their bodies, and eventually makes them explode. If this sounds like something out of a horror movie, you're right. Scientists call this freaky foe a "zombie virus."

This is how the zombie virus works: The virus **infects** a caterpillar and takes over its body. The virus keeps the caterpillar from **molting**. The caterpillar eats and grows bigger, creating more room for the virus to spread.

Then, something freaky happens. The virus forces the caterpillar to crawl up into a tree and remain there until it dies. Its body, which is now mushy, explodes into a virus-filled goo that drips on leaves below. If an unsuspecting caterpillar eats the goo, it happens all over again!

FREAKY FACTS!

A caterpillar infected by the zombie virus becomes soft, black, and goopy. It hangs upside down from a leaf until it explodes!

A TYPE OF WASP PUTS ITS LARVAE INSIDE CATERPILLARS. THE LARVAE EAT THE CATERPILLARS' INSIDES! IN THIS PHOTO, YOU CAN SEE THE LARVAE'S COCOONS OUTSIDE A CATERPILLAR'S BODY.

BEATING THE ZOMBIE

Scientists have learned that a gene called egt is what causes the zombie virus to control a caterpillar's movement. Genes, which are made up of DNA, control an organism's **traits**. In one experiment, scientists removed the egt gene from the zombie virus. Then, they infected caterpillars with the altered virus. The zombie behavior did not happen! When the scientists put the gene back in the virus, the infected caterpillars came under the virus's control.

FROM FLAT TO 3-D

Have you ever printed something from your computer? The image probably comes out flat on a piece of paper. But 3-D printing provides another option: printing real-life, solid objects. This **technology** has created a world of possibilities for manufacturing, design, and some freaky science, too.

Scientists have learned how to make human tissue using a process called bioprinting. The process begins by feeding tiny human cells or other biological matter into a bioprinter, which is a special 3-D printer. The printer creates multiple layers of matter, and these grow into tissue. Scientists think this tissue could one day be used to repair damaged organs such as the liver, kidneys, or lungs—or even replace them. Could the next medical advancement be a 3-D-printed organ? Only time will tell.

FREAKY FACTS!

To date, 3-D printing has successfully created simple body parts like the ear, skin, and the breathing tube we call the trachea.

IS IT FREAKY OR FANTASTIC THAT MACHINES COULD MAKE ORGANS ONE DAY? SCIENTISTS BELIEVE THEY'RE CLOSE TO MAKING THIS A REALITY.

HOW DOES 3-D PRINTING WORK?

3-D printing is more about manufacturing than it is about printing. During this process, materials like plastic are laid down, layer by layer, until an object is created. The printed object comes from a digital file that contains data about each layer. You'll find 3-D printers in manufacturing and design labs, but people have learned to make just about anything, including shoes and cars. NASA (National Aeronautics and Space Administration) even has a 3-D printer to make food on space missions!

SUPER ICE

It's a well-known fact that water freezes into ice. What's less known is that there's a kind of ice that forms at incredibly fast speeds: faster than 1,000 miles per hour (1,609 km/h)! Scientists have known about this "super ice" for some time. It has been found in diamonds from Earth's mantle. However, they never knew how it formed until recently.

This special ice, called Ice VII ("ice seven"), freezes differently than normal ice, and its water molecules create a different pattern of crystals. Using a perfect combination of pressure and temperature, scientists were able to create Ice VII in a lab. They discovered that intense pressure—more than 10,000 times greater than the pressure on Earth's surface—creates super ice. Scientists think this could tell us a lot about water and ice on other planets.

FREAKY FACTS!

Ice VII forms so fast that it could prevent alien life from surviving, if it exists, or from forming in the first place.

THE STUDY OF SOMETHING AS SIMPLE AS ICE COULD GIVE US CLUES ABOUT LIFE ON OTHER PLANETS.

OTHERWORLDLY ICE

The conditions on Earth's surface aren't right for Ice VII, but they could be on other planets such as ocean worlds, which are those covered in liquid water. Although no one knows for sure if ocean worlds exist outside our solar system, they could potentially support life because they have water—unless Ice VII takes over. If a meteor hit an ocean world, it could create conditions needed for super ice to form, reducing the chance for life.

TWO HEADS, ONE BODY

Imagine if someone thousands of miles away could control parts of your body. Pretty weird, right? In 2018, Japanese scientists showed that robots make this possible. Their invention, the Fusion, is a set of robotic arms and a "head" attached to a backpack. It allows two people to work through the same body, at the same time, without being in the same place.

To use the Fusion, one person wears the backpack, and another person remotely controls the robotic limbs with a **virtual reality** (VR) system. The VR operator can see over the wearer's shoulders using the robotic head to observe what they're doing, aiding the wearer or directing the wearer's movement. The operator could even teach the wearer how to play an instrument!

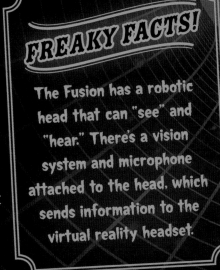

FREAKY FACTS!

The Fusion has a robotic head that can "see" and "hear." There's a vision system and microphone attached to the head, which sends information to the virtual reality headset.

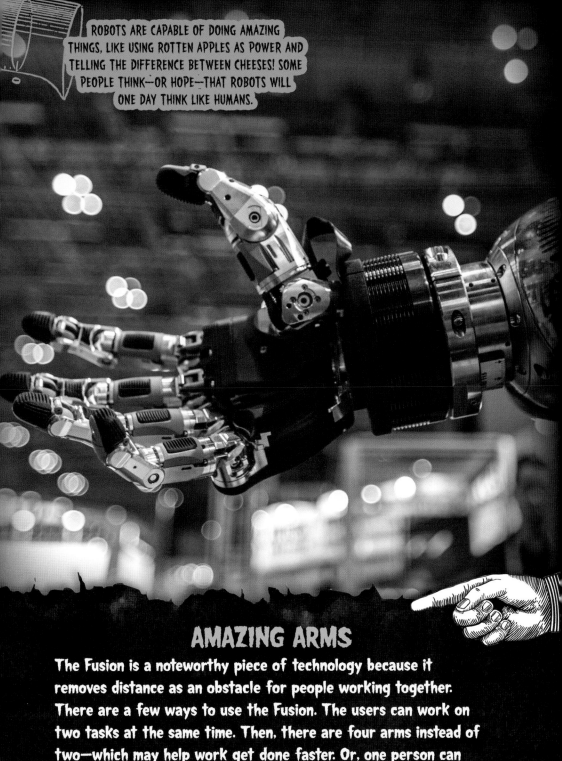

ROBOTS ARE CAPABLE OF DOING AMAZING THINGS, LIKE USING ROTTEN APPLES AS POWER AND TELLING THE DIFFERENCE BETWEEN CHEESES! SOME PEOPLE THINK—OR HOPE—THAT ROBOTS WILL ONE DAY THINK LIKE HUMANS.

AMAZING ARMS

The Fusion is a noteworthy piece of technology because it removes distance as an obstacle for people working together. There are a few ways to use the Fusion. The users can work on two tasks at the same time. Then, there are four arms instead of two—which may help work get done faster. Or, one person can completely control another person's arms and make them move and act however they want.

THE UNIVERSE SPEAKS

Ever since the first black hole was discovered in 1971, these space oddities so far from Earth have continued to puzzle and amaze us. And we can't even see them! However, they're now making themselves heard.

In 2015, a team of US scientists learned they could detect the sound of black holes crashing into each other—1.3 billion **light-years** away! Using a system of lasers, light detectors, and mirrors, the scientists could identify the event's gravitational waves. Then, they turned their measurements into sound waves. That's how, for the first time, we heard the sound of black holes colliding.

So, what does this freaky science sound like? It's been described as a birdlike chirp, the universe "talking," and a "cosmic burp." Gross!

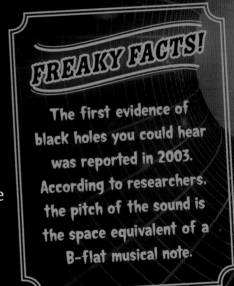

FREAKY FACTS!

The first evidence of black holes you could hear was reported in 2003. According to researchers, the pitch of the sound is the space equivalent of a B-flat musical note.

GREAT GRAVITATIONAL WAVES

In 1916, Albert Einstein predicted that gravitational waves exist in his famous theory of relativity. Massive, accelerating space objects, like black holes orbiting each other, create so much energy that they can actually warp space. Invisible "waves" of energy travel away from the objects at the speed of light—like ripples in a pond. He didn't think the "waves" could be detected on Earth, but this is what scientists measured in 2015.

THIS COMPUTER-PRODUCED IMAGE SHOWS WHAT IT MAY LOOK LIKE WHEN BLACK HOLES SMASH INTO EACH OTHER. THE CURVED LINES REPRESENT HOW GRAVITATIONAL WAVES "BEND" SPACE. THE 2015 DISCOVERY INTRODUCED A WHOLE NEW WAY TO EXPLORE AND UNDERSTAND OUR UNIVERSE.

THE SEWER MONSTER

Where does trash go when it leaves your house? If you lived in London in 2017, it could have become part of a monstrous pile of garbage right beneath your feet!

Meet the fatberg, a trash mass that was 820 feet (250 m) long, twice the size of a soccer field, and about as heavy as a whale. If that isn't freaky enough, consider what it was made of: dirty diapers, cooking oil, grease, wet wipes, and other gross household garbage. It got there by people washing or flushing this trash down their drains. When the trash came together, it formed a solid, hard mass so big that it blocked the sewer system! According to cleanup crews, removing it was like breaking apart concrete.

FREAKY FACTS!

In England, about eight sewer-clogging fatbergs are discovered per week!

THE FATBERG GIVES BACK

Fatbergs are discovered in cities all the time. They happen because of human activity, like flushing trash down the toilet. This practice not only causes fatbergs, but it hurts nature, too. Authorities try to teach people to throw away—not flush—their trash to avoid fatbergs. However, the 2017 sewer monster had a happy ending. Authorities discovered they could separate the fat and oil from the other garbage and turn it into clean fuel.

FLOATING FROGS

Magnets are a perfect example of science at work. With a magnet in your hand, you can pick up all kinds of objects like nails, paper clips ... and frogs?

The famous **levitating** frog is a marvel of science. Frogs, like every other object, are made of tiny particles called atoms, which can be magnetized. Frog atoms aren't naturally a magnet, but they can be. This is what scientists learned when they put a frog inside a tube with a really strong magnetic field. It shifted the properties of the frog's atoms, making the body essentially a magnet. The frog lifted off the ground, attracted to the magnetic field above it. The frog looked like it was floating in midair! Luckily, no frogs were harmed during this discovery.

FREAKY FACTS!

The frog's high water content helped make it a good magnet. Humans are made of a lot of water, too—which means that, in theory, a strong enough magnet could make a person levitate!

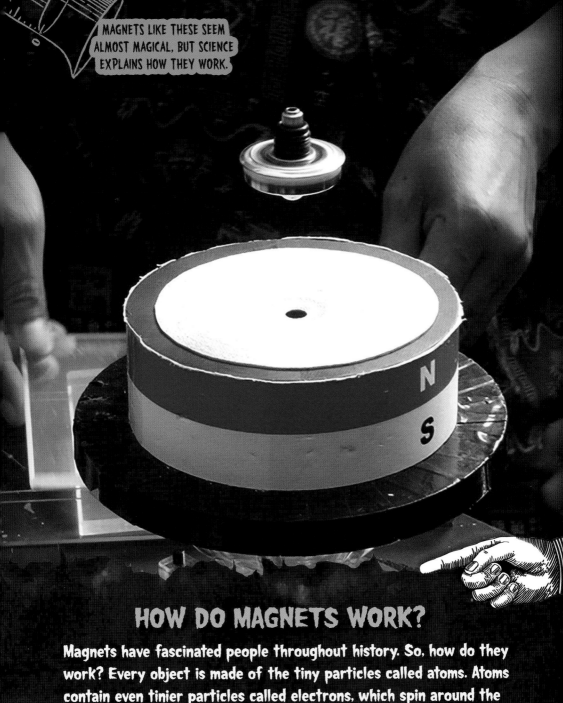

MAGNETS LIKE THESE SEEM ALMOST MAGICAL, BUT SCIENCE EXPLAINS HOW THEY WORK.

HOW DO MAGNETS WORK?

Magnets have fascinated people throughout history. So, how do they work? Every object is made of the tiny particles called atoms. Atoms contain even tinier particles called electrons, which spin around the atom's center. When many electrons spin in the same direction, they create a magnetic force. The opposite ends of a magnet are its north and south poles. Opposite poles attract each other, which is how a magnet can pick up another magnet.

AWE-INSPIRING AURORA

Planet Earth is a wild and wonderful place, with dazzling displays of nature found all over the globe. One of the most famous is the northern lights, or aurora borealis. Patterns of light in shades of pink, blue, green, yellow, purple, and red light up the skies in the far northern area of the globe. This spectacle has been observed since ancient times, but it continues to be one of the weirdest scientific displays out there.

Research has helped us understand the cause of this eerie glow in the sky. When tiny molecules in Earth's atmosphere bump into electrons, **ions**, and other small particles from the sun, they create colorful patterns of light. They can be seen anywhere on Earth, but they're most visible at the poles.

FREAKY FACTS!

Researchers have found evidence that the northern lights move in response to Earth's magnetic field. This movement is why people often describe the lights as "dancing."

CHARGED PARTICLES—OR THOSE WITH AN ELECTRIC CHARGE—TRAVEL FROM THE SUN OUTWARD IN A STREAM CALLED SOLAR WIND. MOST DON'T ENTER EARTH'S ATMOSPHERE, BECAUSE OF THE MAGNETIC FIELD AROUND THE PLANET. THOSE THAT DO ENTER CREATE THE SPECTACULAR LIGHT DISPLAYS.

HOW THE AURORA BOREALIS FORMS

- ELECTRONS HIT AIR MOLECULES
- MOLECULES ARE "EXCITED"
- MOLECULES GIVE OFF LIGHT AS THEY CALM DOWN

ELECTRONS AND IONS

AURORA

SOLAR WIND

SUN

MAGNETIC FIELD LINES

EARTH

AURORA

SOLAR WIND

ELECTRONS AND IONS

THE LEGENDS OF THE NORTHERN LIGHTS

Before science helped uncover the cause of the colorful skies, cultures around the world had explanations for them. The name "aurora" comes from the Roman goddess of dawn's name, because some observers described the phenomenon as looking like daybreak. In the Middle Ages, people thought the northern lights were a sign that war was coming. Some native peoples of North America thought the aurora borealis was the spirits of the dead playing a game with a walrus head.

GLOWING GREEN

Inside Earth's oceans, life can look a little . . . strange. Glowing jellyfish, fish with "headlights," and glimmering worms swim the seas, giving off a green light through something called biofluorescence. It occurs when the green fluorescent protein (GFP) interacts with certain light waves. In 1994, scientists took this freaky phenomenon out of the water and into labs, and cloned it.

Cloning is the process of making a genetic copy of something. As it turns out, cloning GFP is very useful. The GFP gene can be combined with another gene and inserted into cells. It can be tracked by shining **ultraviolet light** on it. This allows scientists to follow cell activity. And watching a virus tagged with GFP shows how quickly and widely it spreads through the body.

FREAKY FACTS!

The GFP gene has been inserted into all kinds of living things, like mice, flies, plants, and pigs. Some people think this "glowing" element makes the organisms more interesting. Others think this is wrong to do to living things.

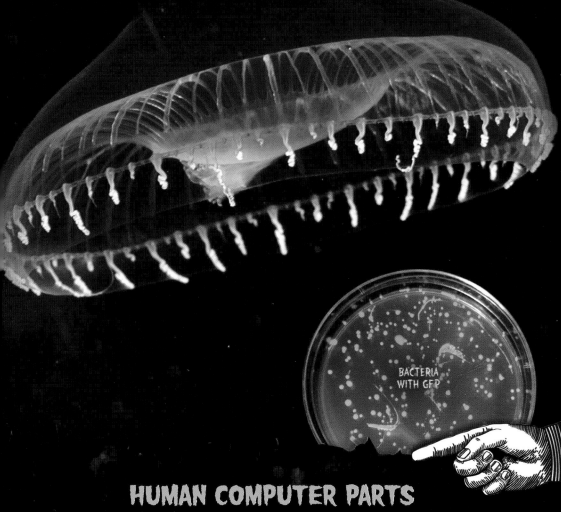

COULD GFP HELP US BETTER UNDERSTAND DISEASES LIKE CANCER? SCIENTISTS ARE WORKING HARD TO CHASE DOWN THE ANSWER.

BACTERIA WITH GFP

HUMAN COMPUTER PARTS

As GFP research shows, scientists are doing some freaky things to learn about the human body! Another amazing idea is DNA computing, or the process of using biological molecules rather than **microprocessors** to make calculations. Scientists have realized there are similarities between DNA, which makes our bodies work, and computer chips. Someday, DNA computers may be able to store billions of times more data and produce much faster calculations than your computer!

POTATO POWER!

The next time you need to turn on a light, find a potato. Believe it or not, this popular food can carry electricity! Potatoes can be used to create a power source because of what they contain. An average potato contains sugar, water, and acid. Certain kinds of metals react with the acid, which creates energy in the form of flowing electrons, or electricity.

To make a battery from a potato, all you need is a zinc **electrode** and a copper electrode. The acid inside the potato forms a chemical reaction with the zinc and copper, and electrons flow from one material to another. Connecting a wire from this "battery" to a light bulb can power the bulb.

BOILED OR MASHED?

In 2010, researchers discovered that a battery made with a boiled potato produced more energy than a battery made with a raw potato. Why? It's all about how freely the electric current can flow. Raw potatoes are pretty stiff, and the electricity has to fight its way through the tough tissue. But boiling breaks down the tissue, which means the electricity can move through it more freely. Simply put, the boiled potato battery creates more power!

27

SCIENCE FOR THE AGES

The amazing thing about science is that there's always a question to answer and something new to discover. Nearly every science discovery was built on a finding that came before it. The efforts to magnetize frogs wouldn't be possible without first understanding how magnets work. Similarly, we wouldn't be listening to black holes today without Einstein's ideas about gravitational waves.

Science is always teaching us something new, and today, we know more than we ever have. Thousands of years ago, our ancestors watched the amazing aurora borealis in the sky just as we do, but now we understand why it happens. This kind of advancement in learning happens every day. It's only a matter of time before the next big discovery!

FREAKY FACTS!

NOAA, the National Oceanic and Atmospheric Administration, has a list of unidentified ocean sounds. There's more to discover underwater!

TWO-HEADED WORMS

Majorly freaky science discoveries happen in the animal kingdom all the time. One of the weirdest happened recently on the International Space Station (ISS): the discovery that a kind of flatworm grows two heads in space! It was already known that these worms can regenerate, or grow back, body parts if they've been cut off. Scientists wanted to see the effect of space on the worms' ability to regenerate. What they found surprised them. The cut worms grew two heads!

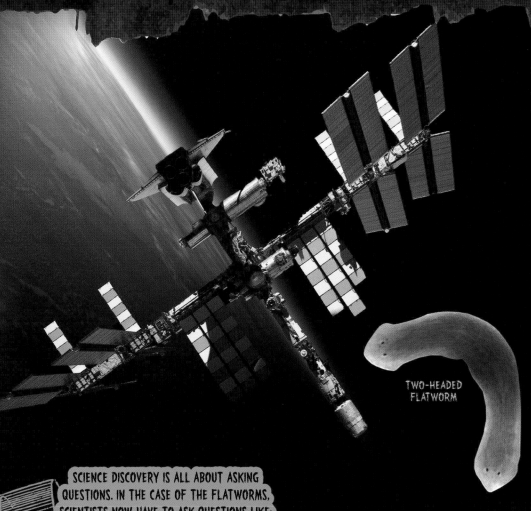

TWO-HEADED
FLATWORM

SCIENCE DISCOVERY IS ALL ABOUT ASKING QUESTIONS. IN THE CASE OF THE FLATWORMS, SCIENTISTS NOW HAVE TO ASK QUESTIONS LIKE: WHAT CONDITION IN SPACE CAUSED THE FLATWORMS TO GROW TWO HEADS?

GLOSSARY

accelerate: to increase in speed

analyze: to study something closely and carefully

electrode: matter through which electricity enters or leaves a circuit

hypothesis: an idea or theory that is not proven but that leads to further study

infect: to spread something harmful inside the body

ion: an atom or group of atoms that has a positive or negative electric charge from losing or gaining one or more electrons

levitate: to cause to rise and float in the air

light-year: the distance light can travel in 1 year

microprocessor: the device in a computer that manages information and controls what the computer does

molt: to leave behind an outer covering that has become too small

technology: tools, machines, or ways to do things that use the latest discoveries to fix problems or meet needs

trait: a feature, such as hair color, that is passed on from parents to children

ultraviolet light: a range of wavelengths in light beyond the violet end of the visible color sequence

virtual reality: an artificial world of images and sounds created by a computer that is affected by the actions of a person who is experiencing it

FOR MORE INFORMATION

BOOKS

Oachs, Emily Rose. *The 12 Most Influential Scientific Discoveries of All Time*. Mankato, MN: 12 Story Library, 2018.

Wood, Matthew Brenden. *The Science of Science Fiction*. White River Junction, VT: Nomad Press, 2017.

WEBSITES

7 Awesome Discoveries Made by Kids
www.livescience.com/47642-discoveries-by-kids.html
Learn about seven cool discoveries made by kids like you.

Famous Scientists
www.dkfindout.com/us/science/famous-scientists/
Read about famous scientists who have advanced our understanding of the world through their awesome discoveries.

Science for Kids
www.natgeokids.com/uk/category/discover/science/
Discover the fascinating world of science through this great site.

INDEX